CENTRAL & SOUTHERN SPAIN NARROW GAUGE

John Organ

MP Middleton Press

Front Cover: The entire population of Calzada appears to be present to witness Couillet 0-6-0 no.3 Belgica engaged in some shunting during the course of a journey from Puertollano to Valdepeñas on 22nd April 1962. (D.Trevor Rowe)

Rear Cover Upper: Couillet 0-6-0T no.5 was recorded hauling a rake of empty skip wagons at Mina Asdrubal on the SMMP 640mm gauge line on 19th September 1962. (D.Trevor Rowe)

Rear Cover Lower: No.201, one of the large 2-6-0s supplied by Robert Stephenson & Hawthorns to the 1067mm gauge Río Tinto Railway in 1953, was viewed outside the depot at the mines complex on 26th April 1962. (D.Trevor Rowe)

Published February 2011

ISBN 978 1 906008 91 8

© Middleton Press, 2011

Design Deborah Esher

Published by
> *Middleton Press*
> *Easebourne Lane*
> *Midhurst*
> *West Sussex*
> *GU29 9AZ*

Tel: 01730 813169
Fax: 01730 812601
Email: info@middletonpress.co.uk
www.middletonpress.co.uk

Printed in the United Kingdom by Henry Ling Limited, at the Dorset Press, Dorchester, DT1 1HD

CONTENTS

ABBREVIATIONS

ESTADO	-	Explotación de Ferrocarriles por el Estado
FEVE	-	Ferrocarriles (del Estado) de Vía Estrecha
MTM	-	La Maquinista Terrestre y Maritima, Barcelona
RENFE	-	Red Nacional de los Ferrocarriles Españoles
SACM	-	Société Alsacienne de Constructions Mécaniques
SECN	-	Sociedad Española de Construcción Naval, Bilbao
SLM	-	Schweizerische Locomotiv-und-Maschinenfabrik, Winterthur
SMMP	-	Sociedad Minera y Metalúrgica de Peñarroya

ACKNOWLEDGEMENTS

The completion of this volume would not have been possible without the assistance of the photographers and other contributors, whose work is contained within these pages. My thanks are therefore due to Dr.Mike Bent, Michael Chapman, Laurence Marshall, Andrew Neale, David Smith, Keith Taylorson, D.Trevor Rowe and Jeremy Wiseman, all of whom have contributed to the successful compilation of material. Thanks are also due to Martyn Knight and Norman Langridge for checking the text in their thorough and efficient manner. Finally, I must as usual thank my wife Brenda, who has shown her usual tolerance and understanding during the period of research and compilation.

INTRODUCTION

In direct contrast to the coastal and mountain regions of Northern Spain, which still boasts an extensive active metre gauge railway network, the central regions of the country are now virtually devoid of any narrow gauge systems. Once blessed with a large variety of railways in gauges ranging from 600mm to 1219mm, which included some very extensive systems, all that now remains is one relatively short electrified metre gauge line to the north of Madrid.

Many of these railways, particularly those in the northern half of central Spain, were short feeder lines which connected with the broad gauge main line network. However in the inland southern half of the country, vast amounts of minerals were mined which required a considerable network of railways to provide transport to the ports situated on the Gulf of Cadiz.

Although the majority of the narrow gauge railways in this large area were independent operations, some were transferred to State ownership and operated by ESTADO during the later years of their active lives. Ironically only one narrow gauge line was incorporated into the State owned RENFE after its formation in 1941, this being the only narrow gauge line to have survived in central Spain. Many of the lines suffered heavy losses during the Spanish Civil War, whilst subsequent repairs were delayed as a result of the rest of Europe being pre-occupied with World War II.

This album will attempt to portray the enormous variety of narrow gauge systems that were once a part of everyday life in the central part of this large country of contrasts; contrasts that range from the windswept plains of Castile, via the capital city of Madrid to the desolate industrial landscape of Huelva.

I.   The Iberian Peninsula showing the locations of the railways featured. The numbers refer to the section headings.

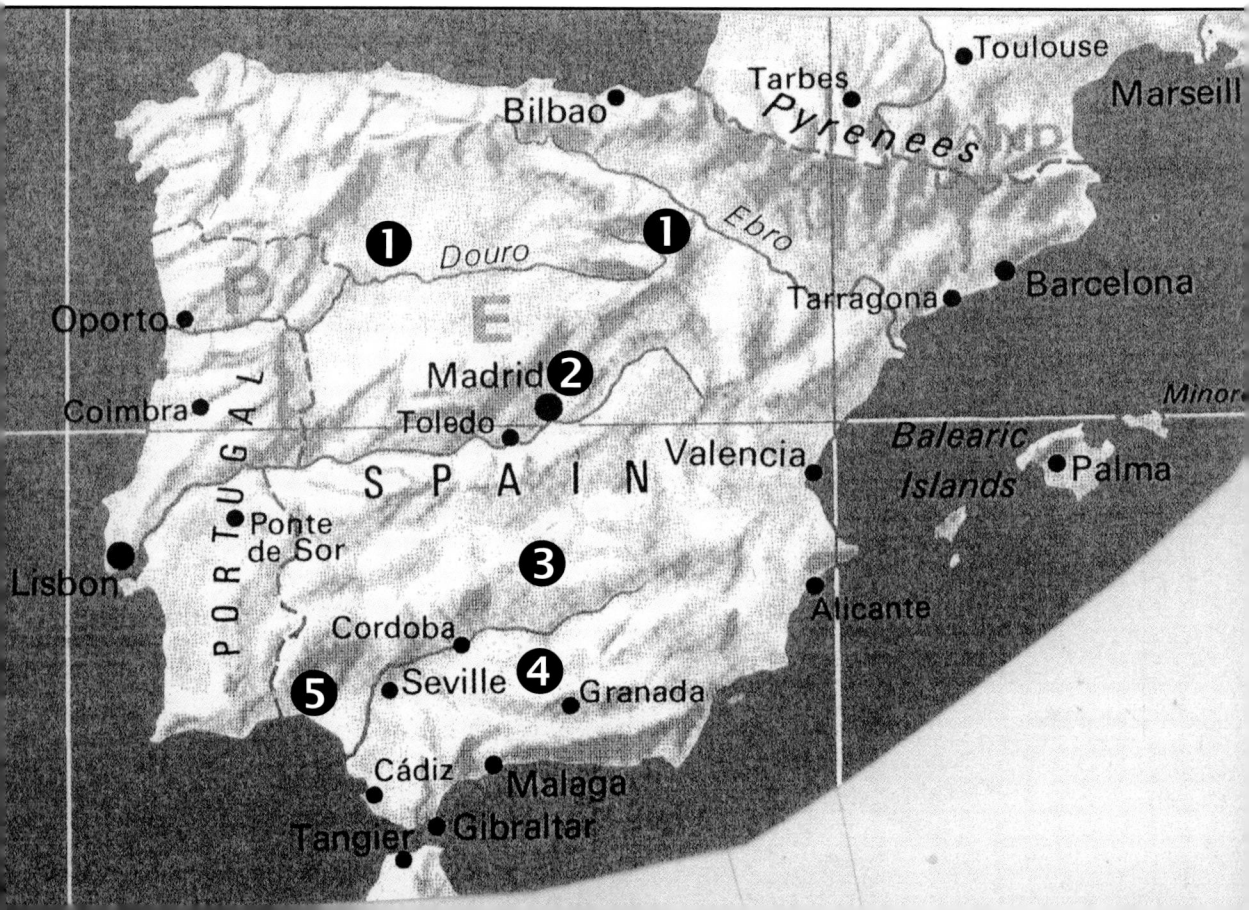

1. Castile to Aragón

The broad sweep of the central plain of Spain, situated to the south of the Cantábrica and Pyrenees mountain chain, was once the location of a large number of metre gauge railways. Two of these were quite extensive systems whilst the remainder comprised short feeder lines to the important RENFE main line route which linked the Atlantic and Mediterranean coasts. During their heyday these lines transported both large numbers of passengers and much heavy freight, whilst the smaller lines were among the first in the country to introduce railcars for their passenger services. Sadly all were closed during the 1960s as a result of competition from road transport and rationalisation of the railway network.

II. The full extent of the Castilian Secondary Railways system is shown. (Dr M.Bent)

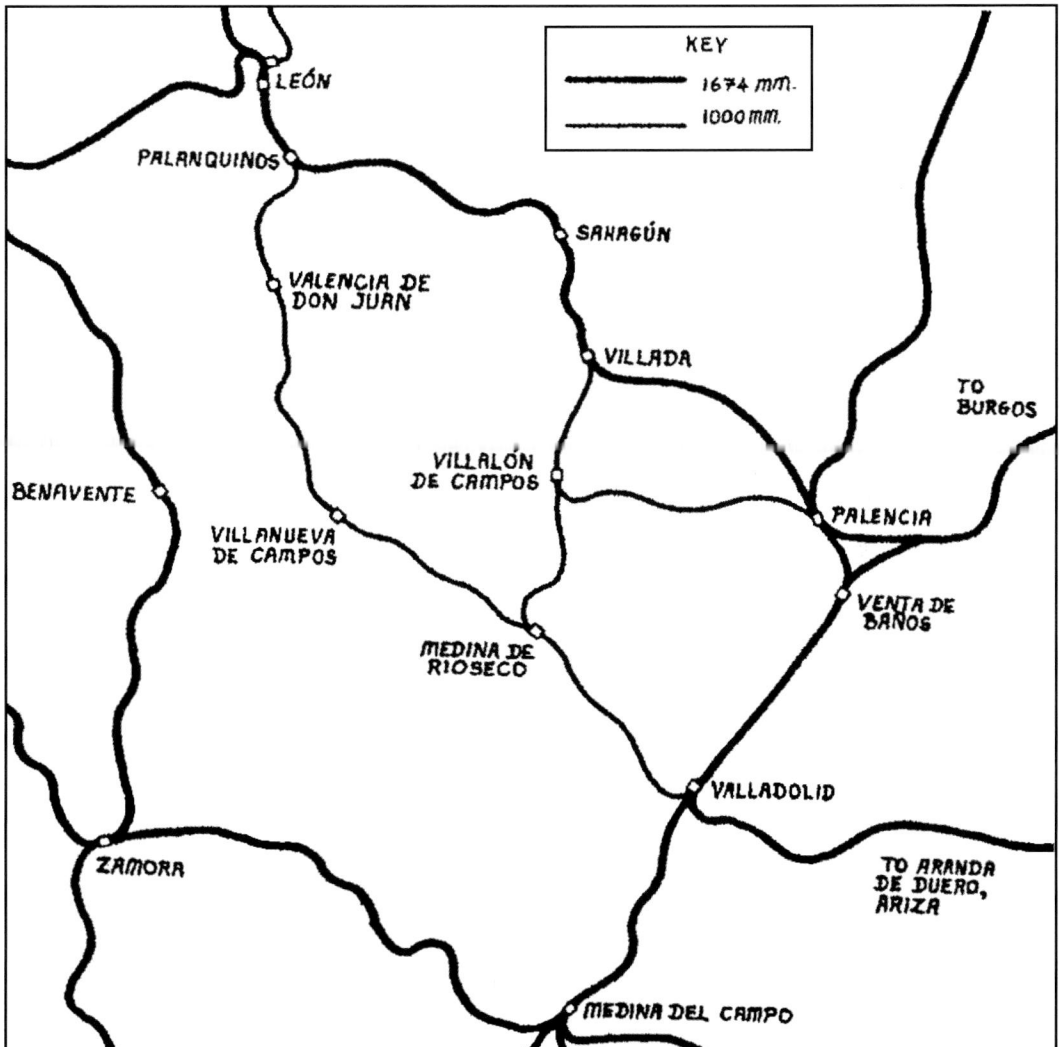

CASTILIAN SECONDARY RAILWAYS (FSC)

The windswept plain of Castile, to the northwest of Madrid, was traversed by an extensive metre gauge system with a total length of 230km known as the Compañia de Ferrocarriles de Castilla y Española de Ferrocarriles Secundarios (FSC), a name that evolved following the merger of two companies in 1932. Although the headquarters of the FSC was situated at Palencia, the original section of the network was from Valladolid to Medina de Rioseco, a distance of 42km which opened in 1884. The line was eventually extended by a further 87km in 1912, when Medina de Rioseco was connected to Villada and Palencia, this section being opened by King Alfonso VIII. The final 101km linking Medina de Rioseco and Palanquinos at the northern extremity of the system was completed in 1915. Connection with the main line system (RENFE after 1941) was made at Valladolid, Palencia, Villada and Palanquinos.

The original motive power was provided by six Sharp Stewart 0-4-0T tramway locomotives adorned with enclosed wheels and motion, which were supplied in 1884. These small machines manfully operated the services over the undulating route of the original section until 1911, when they were joined by seven 2-6-0Ts built in Barcelona by MTM, with a further six similar machines being added to the fleet in 1913. These powerful locomotives remained in service for the rest of the line's existence, whilst some Billard type A150-D7 railcars arrived in 1960 for use on the passenger services during the latter years of the operation. Two of the original 0-4-0Ts, with their tramway appendages removed, remained in service until closure for shunting duties and for haulage over the 3km long tramway through the streets of Valladolid. This section, which linked the centrally situated station at Campo de Béjar to the original station at San Bartolomé on the outskirts of Valladolid, was in later years used only during the hours of darkness in order to avoid undue traffic congestion.

The FSC was taken over by ESTADO in 1965, the new owners quickly realising that the operation was no longer a financially viable proposition. As a consequence the FSC was closed in 1969, road transport subsequently providing connections with the RENFE network.

1.1.   One of the original Sharp Stewart 0-4-0Ts supplied to the Castilian Secondary Railways, no.6 *Rioseco*, was seen simmering outside the shed at Valladolid on 4th April 1954. (D.Trevor Rowe)

1.2.   MTM 2-6-0T no.8 of the FSC was recorded prior to departing from Valladolid with a mixed train bound for Palencia on 22nd March 1965. (D.Trevor Rowe)

1.3.   A few minutes later no.8 was witnessed as it hauled its train alongside the cobbled street in the outskirts of Valladolid. (D.Trevor Rowe)

1.4.   At the same location, one of the Billard A150-D7 railcars was photographed as it arrived with a passenger service from Palencia. Note the trailer car and one of the earlier bogie carriages attached to the rear. (D.Trevor Rowe)

1.5.   2-6-0T no.8 also features in this view at Villanubla as the locomotive paused for attention to its valve motion during the course of a journey from Valladolid to Medina de Rioseco on 13th May 1962. (L.G.Marshall)

1.6.   The grass strewn tracks at Medina de Rioseco was the location of this scene featuring 2-6-0T no.4 as it departed with a mixed train bound for Palanquinos on the same occasion. (L.G.Marshall)

1.7.   Sister locomotive no.9 was also recorded at Medina de Rioseco during the course of a journey from Palanquinos to Valladolid on 13th May 1962. (L.G.Marshall)

1.8.   The depot at Palencia was the location for this view of 2-6-0T no.2, as it awaited its next turn of duty, on 16th September 1963. (D.Trevor Rowe)

1.9.   The windswept plains of Castile provided the backdrop for this view of 2-6-0T no.8 when it was witnessed near Villalón whilst en route to Palencia on 9th March 1968, during the final year of the FSC. (J.Wiseman)

1.10.   Shortly prior to the closure of the FSC, Sharp Stewart 0-4-0T no.6 *Rioseco*, masquerading as no.1 *Valladolid*, and an attendant carriage were photographed on static display at Valladolid in March 1968. (J.Wiseman)

HARO-EZCARAY RAILWAY

Although the majority of the RENFE broad gauge routes radiated from Madrid, there was one notable exception in the former Norte line that linked Bilbao on the north coast to Tarragona on the Mediterranean coast. A number of metre gauge "feeder" lines connected with this important route as it followed the valley of the Río Ebro for much of its journey through Castile and Aragón. The first to be encountered was the 34km long line that connected with the RENFE route at Haro and ran south to Ezcaray. Opened as late as 1916, the short line incorporated a substantial deep cutting and an impressive viaduct at Haro before heading across open countryside to the southern terminus. Whilst operating a basic rural service for almost 50 years, economics dictated that it was no longer a financially viable concern, even ESTADO considered it not worth taking over. As a consequence the line was closed in March 1964.

Motive power throughout the line's existence comprised three North British 4-4-0Ts dating from 1906, which were acquired secondhand from the FC de Carreño at Gijón. Passenger services during the later years of the operation were in the main provided by Wismar type 4-wheel railcars, a number of these German designed vehicles being assembled in Spain during the 1930s.

III.   The narrow gauge lines which connected with the RENFE route along the Río Ebro are shown in this diagram of the full extent of the network prior to the first closures as described in the text. (Dr.M.Bent)

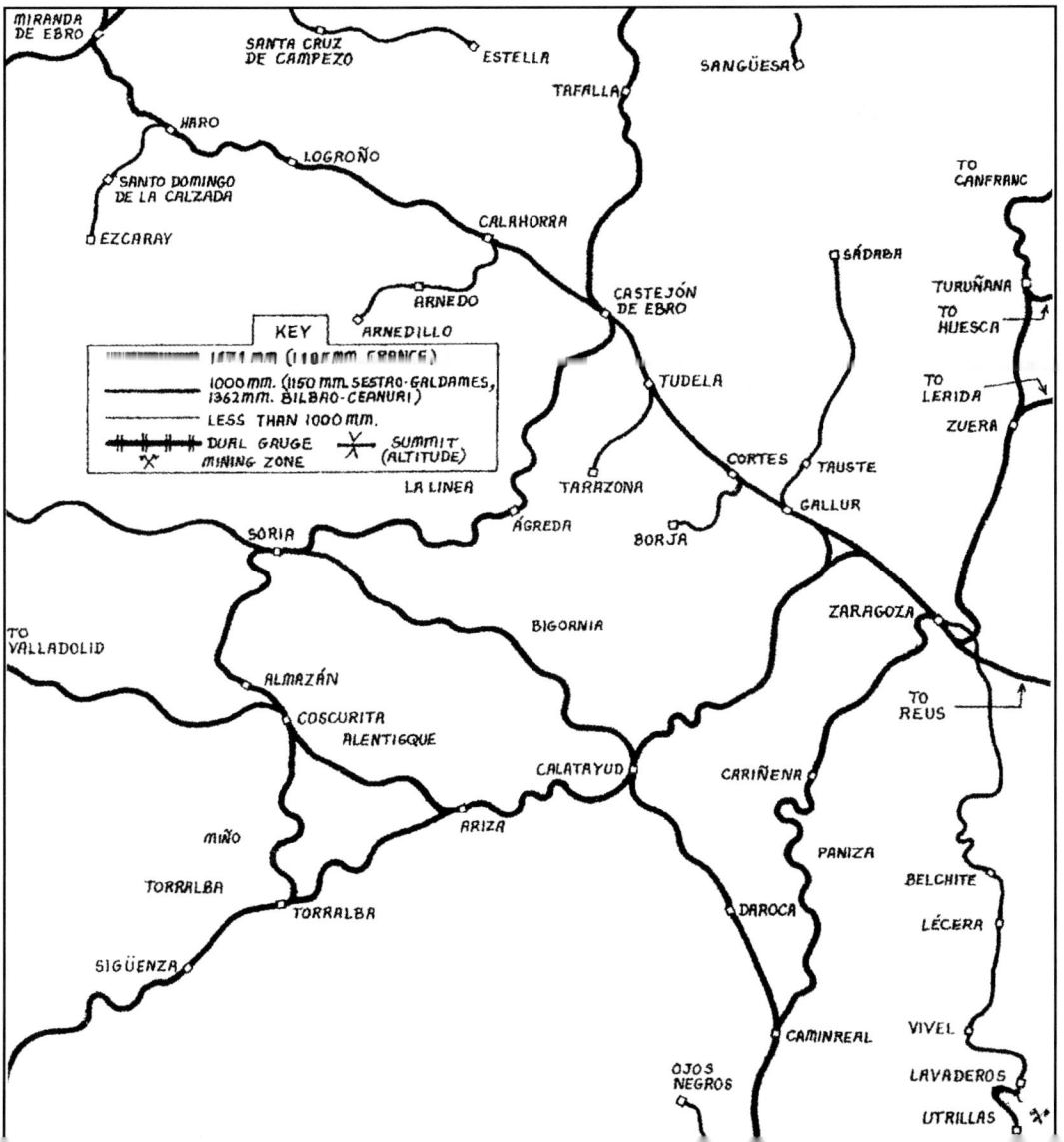

1.11.   North British 4-4-0T no.3 *Villanueva* was recorded whilst engaged in shunting operations at Haro on 16th September 1963. (D.Trevor Rowe)

CALAHORRA - ARNEDILLO

Having passed from Castile into Aragón during the course of our journey along the valley of the Río Ebro, the next metre gauge line to be encountered was at the historic 14th century cathedral town of Calahorra. This is another line that ran in a southerly direction to a terminus at Arnedillo, a distance of 36km. Construction began in 1922 but the final 4km was delayed by the onset of the Civil War in 1935. Arnedillo was finally connected in 1947, by which time the line had been taken over by ESTADO. Despite the disruptions caused during the war and its aftermath, the line provided a useful service until the "march of progress" caught up during the 1960s. Closure eventually occurred in 1966, when the competition from road transport proved to be unassailable.

The original locomotives were three war surplus Baldwin 2-6-0Ts dating from 1916. However these were ultimately replaced by two of the large 2-8-2Ts built in 1933 at Trubia for the FC de Ferrol a Gijón (see *Northern Spain Narrow Gauge*), which were more than adequate for handling the amount of traffic on offer. In 1952 they were joined by a Couillet 0-6-0T from the nearby Tudela-Tarazona line, which had been taken over and converted to broad gauge by RENFE. Railcars arrived on the scene during the 1930s in the form of three Wismar 4-wheel vehicles. These were subsequently rebuilt and modified in the workshops at Calahorra in order to provide a more efficient service during the final years of the operation of this short metre gauge railway.

1.12.   Still retaining its FG ownership plate, Trubia 2-8-2T no.1 was photographed at Arnedo, which was the half way point of the Calahorra-Arnedillo line, on 6th April 1963. (J.Wiseman)

1.13.   Couillet 0-6-0T no.32 *Cascante* was in charge of a freight train heading for Arnedillo when it was recorded near Arnedo on 4th October 1963. (D.Trevor Rowe)

1.14.   One of the Wismar railcars, which had been rebuilt and modified at Calahorra, was seen in action at Arnedo on 10th April 1965. (J.Wiseman)

GALLUR - SÁDABA

The longest of the metre gauge "feeder" lines along this important broad gauge route was the only one to proceed in a northerly direction. The 56km long Ferrocarril de Sádaba a Gallur, which connected the two towns, was opened in 1915 and led an undistinguished life until it succumbed in 1970. Rather surprisingly it remained an independent operation throughout this period, not having been taken over by the state owned ESTADO, unlike many of its contemporaries. The route progressed through the fairly mundane countryside typical of this area of Spain, with little in the way of any notable civil engineering structures to enliven the scene.

Motive power was provided from the outset by four 0-6-0Ts built in Barcelona by MTM, which were joined by another identical locomotive in 1927. Passenger services were provided by three Wismar railcars after 1935, whilst during the final decade a Spanish built diesel-hydraulic Bo-Bo locomotive was used to supplement the surviving steam locomotives. Freight traffic, as with the other lines, consisted of general merchandise and agricultural commodities.

A short distance from Gallur was another metre gauge line linking Cortes to Borja, 7km to the south. Opened in 1889, this short line closed in 1955 although two Manning Wardle 0-6-0Ts and a similar locomotive built by St.Leonard, Liége remained in store at Cortes for almost another decade.

1.15.   The depot at Gallur, with the turntable in the foreground, was photographed on 10th April 1965. Two of the MTM 0-6-0Ts can be seen inside the shed, whilst sundry items of rolling stock are also featured in this view. (J.Wiseman)

1.16.   WMG1, a Wismar 4-wheel railcar, was also recorded at Gallur depot on the same occasion. Unlike the railcars at Calahorra, those at Gallur retained their original appearance. (J. Wiseman)

1.17.   During the final decade of the line's existence, the majority of the freight trains were hauled by the newly delivered diesel-hydraulic locomotive. This typical combination was viewed at Ejea de los Caballeros on 14th February 1967. (J. Wiseman)

ZARAGOZA - UTRILLAS

Zaragoza, the largest town to be encountered along the Río Ebro route, was once the northern terminal of two metre gauge lines, including one of the most legendary of Spanish narrow gauge lines.

The Utrillas Railway, or the Cia.de Minas y Ferrocarril de Utrillas (MFU) as it was officially known in Spain, included a 126km long metre gauge line that linked Zaragoza and the coal mining area centred near Utrillas. Opened in 1904 principally as a coal carrying line, a limited passenger service was also provided. In 1954 the daily "correo" required 5 hours 44 minutes to complete the journey, which doubtless made many stops en route.

From the enthusiast point of view, the major attraction of the Utrillas operation was the impressive motive power used on the line. Originally provided with a batch of ten O & K 2-6-0Ts, most of which survived until closure, these were subsequently joined by various second hand machines including 0-4-4-0T and 0-6-6-0T Mallets plus Belgian 0-6-0Ts and two Spanish 2-6-2Ts constructed by MTM in 1926. Apart from some of the original 2-6-0Ts, these had all departed by the early 1950s. They were replaced initially by four of the highly successful 1903/6 built Krauss 2-6-0 + 4 "Engerth" locomotives from the FFCC Vascongados (see *Northern Spain Narrow Gauge*). However the MFU was best known during its last decade for the fleet of eleven immense SACM 2-6-6-0T Mallets purchased from Tunisia during the early 1950s. These powerful locomotives dating from 1922/3 provided the mainstay of the motive power requirements following their arrival. Used for both freight and passenger operations, their sheer power proved to be invaluable when hauling heavy fully laden coal trains along the undulating and steeply graded route from the mines at Utrillas to the RENFE transhipment point at Zaragoza.

At Utrillas, the MFU also had a 600mm system at the mines complex which was operated by O & K 0-4-0WT and Henschel 0-4-0T locomotives. As with the metre gauge "main" line of the system, a passenger service was also provided on the 600mm section, principally for colliery workers. Two of the O & K 0-4-0WTs are now domiciled in the UK at the West Lancashire Light Railway, whilst a Henschel 0-4-0T now works on the South Tynedale Railway.

The entire system of the MFU was taken over by ESTADO in 1963. However their period of control was brief, the system being closed in 1966. By that time passenger services had dwindled to one train in each direction three times per week, the journey time for which had increased to over seven hours.

Zaragoza was also formerly the northern terminal of another metre gauge railway. This was the 48km long FC de Cariñena a Zaragoza, which began operations in 1887. After a relatively short life it closed in 1933, being replaced by a new broad gauge route. One of the Sharp Stewart 0-6-0Ts, supplied between 1885 and 1888, survived the fate of being scrapped and was sent to Las Palmas in the Canary Islands.

1.18.   Two of the O & K 2-6-0Ts, with no.2 in the lead, were recorded at Zaragoza upon arrival with a freight train from Utrillas on 10th June 1954. (D.Trevor Rowe)

1.19.   One of the Krauss 2-6-0 + 4 "Engerth" locomotives transferred from Northern Spain is featured in this view of no.104 at Zaragoza on 10th April 1965. The frames of the articulated tender extending under the cab can be clearly seen. (J.Wiseman)

1.20.   Ex-Tunisian SACM 2-6-6-0T Mallet no.202 was viewed as it passed a passenger train at Lécera, whilst hauling a southbound freight train on 5th April 1961. (D.Trevor Rowe)

1.21.   The desolate surroundings of Azuara were the location for this scene featuring O & K 2-6-0T no.6 and Mallet no.204 as they hauled a heavy train towards Zaragoza on 8th April 1961. (D.Trevor Rowe)

1.22.　2-6-6-0T Mallet no.204 was recorded marshalling the fully laden wagons of a coal train at Utrillas on the same occasion. (D.Trevor Rowe)

1.23.　2-6-0T no.7 was engaged in shunting operations at Utrillas when it was photographed at the extensive mining complex on 8th April 1961. (D.Trevor Rowe)

1.24.   The sheer bulk of the SACM 2-6-6-0T Mallets can be appreciated in this view of no.204 as it was being prepared for its 126km long journey from Utrillas to Zaragoza on 8th April 1961. (D.Trevor Rowe)

1.25.   The semi-roundhouse at the depot of the 600mm system at Utrillas was also viewed on the same occasion. Three O & K 0-4-0WTs and a Henschel 0-4-0T were seen between duties. (D.Trevor Rowe)

1.26.   Inside the shed, 0-4-0WT no.4 was standing above a pit, whilst a hose was draped across the front buffer beam. (D.Trevor Rowe)

1.27.   Outside the depot, 0-4-0T no.11 was coupled to a short four wheel carriage used by the miners at the colliery. (D.Trevor Rowe)

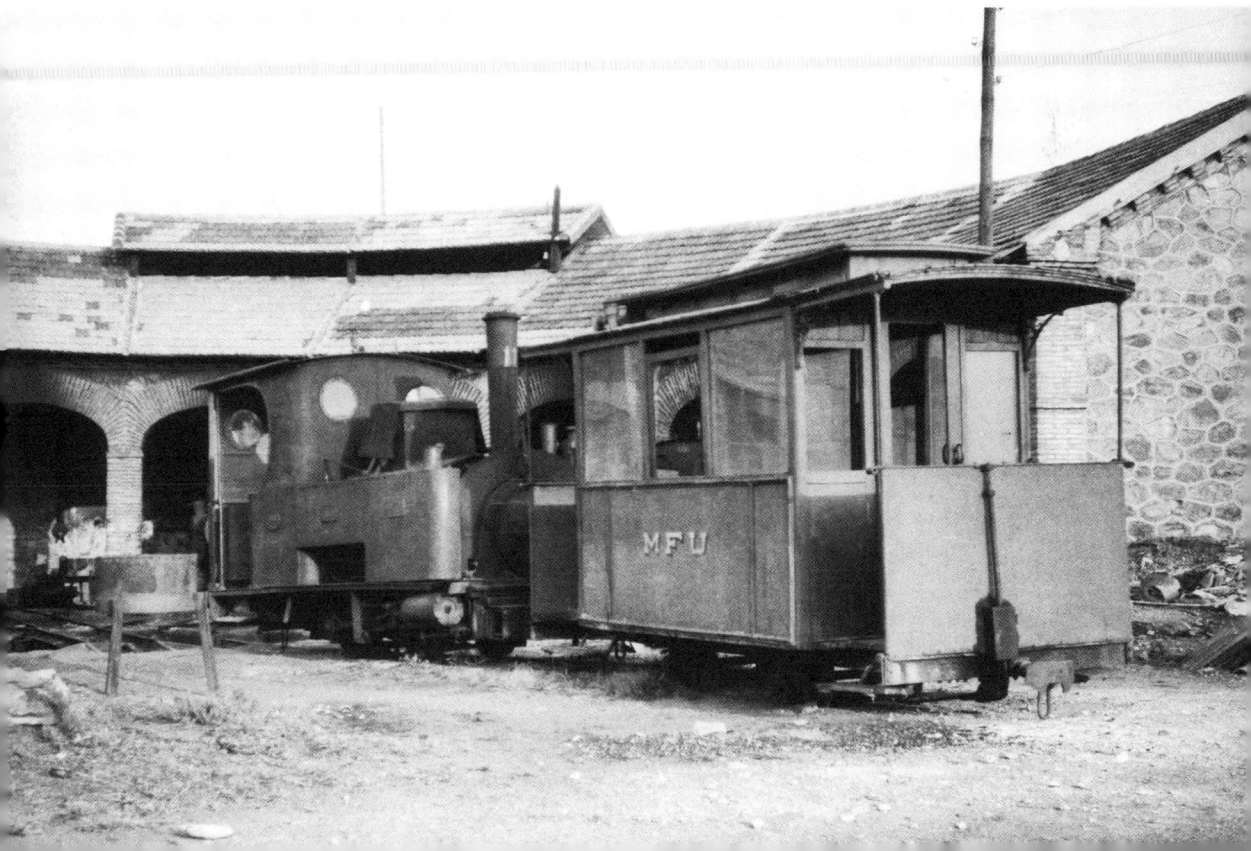

1.28.   O & K 0-4-0WT no.22 *Montalban* currently resides at the West Lancashire Light Railway. It was recorded during a visit to the Welsh Highland Heritage Railway in May 2010, whilst hauling a demonstration freight train. (M.Chapman)

1.29.   No.32, a Henschel 0-4-0T from the Utrillas mines system is based at the South Tynedale Railway. Now named *Thomas Edmondson*, the 1918 built locomotive was viewed inside the workshop at Alston during June 2010. (M.Chapman)

2. Narrow Gauge Around Madrid

At an elevation of 650m above sea level, Madrid is the highest capital city in Europe. It is also one of the most centrally situated, which proved to be advantageous when the initial plans for a main line railway system were drawn up. This central position allowed for a series of broad gauge routes radiating from the capital city, although later additions saw important cross country routes added to the network.

Madrid was also served by two metre gauge lines that terminated within the city, whilst two other metre gauge lines plus a short 600mm line were located to the north. One of the northern metre gauge lines is the only surviving narrow gauge line in Central Spain.

IV.   The full extent of the narrow gauge lines in the area around Madrid are depicted in this map. Only one of these lines has survived, this being the electrified route serving Los Cotos. (D.H.Smith)

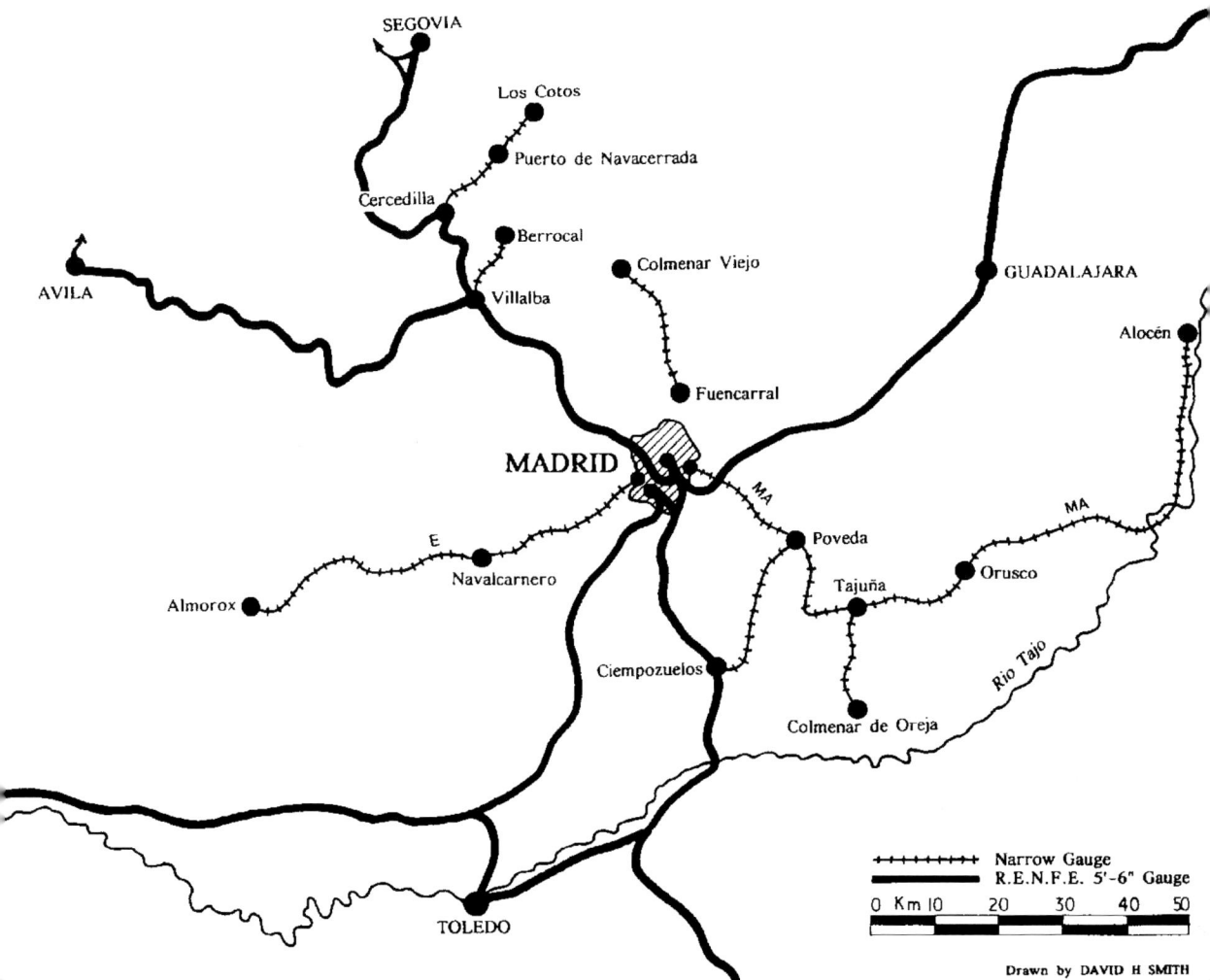

MADRID - ARAGÓN RAILWAY

Despite its name, the Cia. del Ferrocarril de Madrid a Aragón (MA) never succeeded in reaching its ultimate destination of Caminreal in Aragón. The initial stage of the route running from Madrid Niño Jesus station in an easterly direction to Tajuña opened in 1886, to which were added branches from Poveda to Ciempozuelos and Tajuña to Colmenar de Oreja. In 1919 the first stage of the proposed extension to Caminreal was opened as far as Alocén, 142km from Madrid. This proved to be final extent of the MA system.

Although passenger traffic was catered for, the MA was mainly a freight operation. One of the principal commodities carried was lime, along with sugar and other agricultural products together with general merchandise.

Initially the motive power was provided by a fleet of 0-6-0Ts, most of which were supplied by the Belgian manufacturer Haine St.Pierre (HSP) between 1886 and 1912. There were also two similar Kerr Stuart 0-6-0Ts supplied in 1904. When the line was extended to Alocén in 1919 more powerful locomotives were deemed to be necessary, especially with the proposed continuation of the route to Caminreal in mind. The result was the arrival of three HSP 2-6-6-0 Mallets in that year, which handled the heavy freight trains for the next four decades. These were massive tender locomotives and were more than equal to the tasks demanded of them. Finally in 1952, two 2-6-2Ts were supplied by MTM at Barcelona, principally for passenger train haulage. However the passenger service was withdrawn in 1955, following which the two MTM locomotives were subsequently rebuilt as 2-6-4Ts and used for freight haulage.

Apart from the 26km section linking Poveda to the RENFE at Ciempozuelos, the MA was closed in stages during the 1960s. The surviving section provided access to the sugar factory at Poveda, which once also boasted an internal 600mm gauge system. Poveda is now connected to the RENFE by a broad gauge connection, whilst the southern section of the line has been converted to broad gauge by the Portland Valderrivas company for the transport of lime and cement, trains being hauled by General Electric diesel locomotives.

2.1.   A poor record of one of the original locomotives of the MA, HSP 0-6-0T no.2 of 1886, features in this view at Madrid Niño depot on 6th June 1954. (D.Trevor Rowe)

2.2.   Some intricate shunting operations were taking place when 0-6-0T no.13 was captured at the same location in September 1955. This was one of the later HSP locomotives, constructed in 1905. (K.Taylorson coll.)

2.3.   By contrast to the earlier 0-6-0Ts, the three 2-6-6-0 Mallets supplied by HSP to the MA in 1919 were massive locomotives. No.202 is pictured as it was raising steam at Poveda on 18th September 1961. (D.Trevor Rowe)

2.4.   Another view of no.202, which emphasises the bulk of these machines, was obtained on the same occasion. Although not officially recorded as such, they appear to have been oil fired judging by the construction of the tender. (D.Trevor Rowe)

MADRID - ALMOROX RAILWAY

Terminating at the centrally situated Madrid Goya station, the metre gauge Ferrocarril de Madrid a Almorox ran in a westerly direction for 74km through typically Spanish rural scenery. The first stage to Navalcarnero was opened in 1891, being extended to Almorox in 1901. At one stage ambitious plans were considered to extend the line further west towards to Extremadura, within striking distance of the Portuguese border. On the outskirts of Madrid the line served the large military base at Cuatro Vientos, which boasted a substantial internal system comprising both broad gauge and 600mm rails.

From the time of its opening the motive power most commonly associated with the line were the ten Krauss 0-6-0Ts supplied between 1890 and 1912. These were ultimately joined by three 1922 MTM 2-6-2Ts from the Vasco-Navarro railway in the north of the country, along with a Nasmyth Wilson 2-6-0T of 1892 vintage from the same source. Bogie carriages were also transferred from the northern line to supplement the original four wheeled vehicles.

The line was taken over by ESTADO in 1930, who were instrumental in transferring the larger locomotives and bogie carriages from the, by then, electrified Vasco-Navarro line in an attempt to improve the journey times. The final acceleration of the passenger services occurred in 1959 when Billard railcars were introduced, cutting the journey time by one hour. Sadly their arrival was too late to save the line, services being cut back to Navalcarnero in 1966 before it closed completely in 1970. A section of the trackbed on the outskirts of Madrid has been converted to broad gauge and incorporated into the RENFE suburban network.

2.5.   The depot at Madrid Goya was the location for a view of three Krauss 0-6-0Ts, nos 9, 1 and 3 together with a Nasmyth Wilson 2-6-0T on 30th May 1955. (D.Trevor Rowe)

2.6.   Krauss 0-6-0T no.4 *Alberche* was also recorded at Goya depot in April 1955. These small locomotives were indelibly associated with the Almorox line until they were joined by larger locomotives during the ESTADO era. (J.Wiseman)

2.7.   Former Vasco-Navarro Railway MTM 2-6-2T no.14 features in this view of one of the later additions to the fleet at Goya depot on 30th May 1955. (D.Trevor Rowe)

2.8.   0-6-0T no.4 was captured as it departed from Madrid Goya station with a short passenger train bound for Almorox on 6th June 1954. (D.Trevor Rowe)

2.9. Krauss 0-6-0T no.5 *Villadelprado* was recorded near Cuatro Vientos as it hauled the afternoon passenger service to Almorox during March 1955. (J.Wiseman)

2.10. Back at Madrid Goya, MTM 2-6-2T no.15 was still in service during the final period of operation of the Almorox line. This view was obtained on 18th April 1964, prior to the closure of the western section beyond Navalcarnero. (J.Wiseman)

FUENCARRAL - COLMENAR VIEJO

Situated on the northern outskirts of Madrid, Fuencarral was the southern terminus of a 23km long metre gauge line that ran to Colmenar Viejo (which translates to The Old Apiary). Operated by ESTADO as an isolated branch of the Madrid-Almorox, the track was laid along the route of a former standard gauge tramway. The city tramway network extended to Fuencarral and provided a cross platform connection with the metre gauge line after its conversion in 1943.

Locomotives and rolling stock were supplied by the Almorox line, being transferred across the city by road when the need arose. Normally two of the Krauss 0-6-0Ts were based at Fuencarral, whilst a single bogie carriage was deemed adequate for the service on offer which invariably operated as mixed trains. Occasionally one of the 2-6-2Ts was used to provide haulage, however this was a rare occurrence.

Throughout its short life, traffic on the line was light and was obviously not an economically sound operation. As a consequence ESTADO closed the line in April 1955.

2.11.   Krauss 0-6-0T no.2 *Guadarrama* was in service when it was photographed at Fuencarral whilst departing with a typical mixed train bound for Colmenar Viejo, with a vintage style bogie carriage providing the passenger accommodation, on 29th May 1955. (D.Trevor Rowe)

2.12.   During the return journey on the same occasion, no.2 was recorded as it approached Fuencarral amid the sweeping plains to the north of Madrid. (D.Trevor Rowe)

2.13.   The station and depot complex at Colmenar Viejo was the location for this view of 0-6-0T no.10 Almorox in May 1955. This was the last of the Krauss locomotives to be supplied to the Almorox line, having arrived in 1912. (D.Trevor Rowe)

CERCEDILLA - LOS COTOS

Although the narrow gauge lines under state control were normally operated by ESTADO, two exceptions were the two RENFE lines to the north of Madrid. One of these is still active and providing a useful service, whilst the other was an early casualty. This was the 11km long 600mm gauge line that ran between Villalba and Berrocal, the ballast quarries at the latter location being its major source of revenue. Opened in 1882, this short line relied on two Corpet-Louvet 0-6-0Ts for its entire existence until 1957 when the line closed, being considered to be no longer economic.

By complete contrast, the 1500v metre gauge FC Eléctrico del Guadarrama remains in use as the only narrow gauge line under RENFE control. The initial 11km to Puerto de Navacerrada were opened in 1923 by the Spanish King and Queen. The line was closed during the duration of the Civil War (1936-39) and was re-opened in 1941, following the nationalisation of the Spanish Railway network and formation of RENFE in that year. In 1964 the route was extended a further 7km to Los Cotos, a popular ski resort situated at an elevation of 1830m. The original voltage of 1200v DC was raised to 1500v in 1973.

The line remains a popular destination for winter sports enthusiasts, whilst during the summer months it provides a well used service for the many hikers who visit the area. Being located so near to Madrid, the line provides a convenient "escape" from the traffic congested and polluted atmosphere of the city.

The original equipment supplied in 1923 consisted of Swiss built EMUs, some of which were still in operation until the recent past. In 1964 a small fleet of Spanish built SECN "Naval" units, similar to those supplied to various ESTADO and FEVE lines, were acquired to replace the ageing Swiss machines. However, these proved to be deficient in their braking efficiency on the steeply graded route. This was highlighted during a test run of one of the units, which accelerated out of control during the descent, reaching a speed of 60kph before it was brought under control on the approach to the station at Cercedilla. As a consequence of this "near disaster", the "Naval" units were transferred to the Catalonia system whilst the venerable Swiss units maintained the service a little longer. In 1976 the first of an updated version of the Swiss designed units, built by MTM Barcelona was supplied. The success of this vehicle led to the introduction of a fleet of similar MTM built units during the following decade, which are still in use on this scenic and well used line.

2.14.   The extensive station complex at Cercedilla, with its cross platform interchange with the RENFE broad gauge lines, features one of the Swiss EMUs as it awaited departure with a service to Los Cotos on 23rd March 1965. (D.Trevor Rowe)

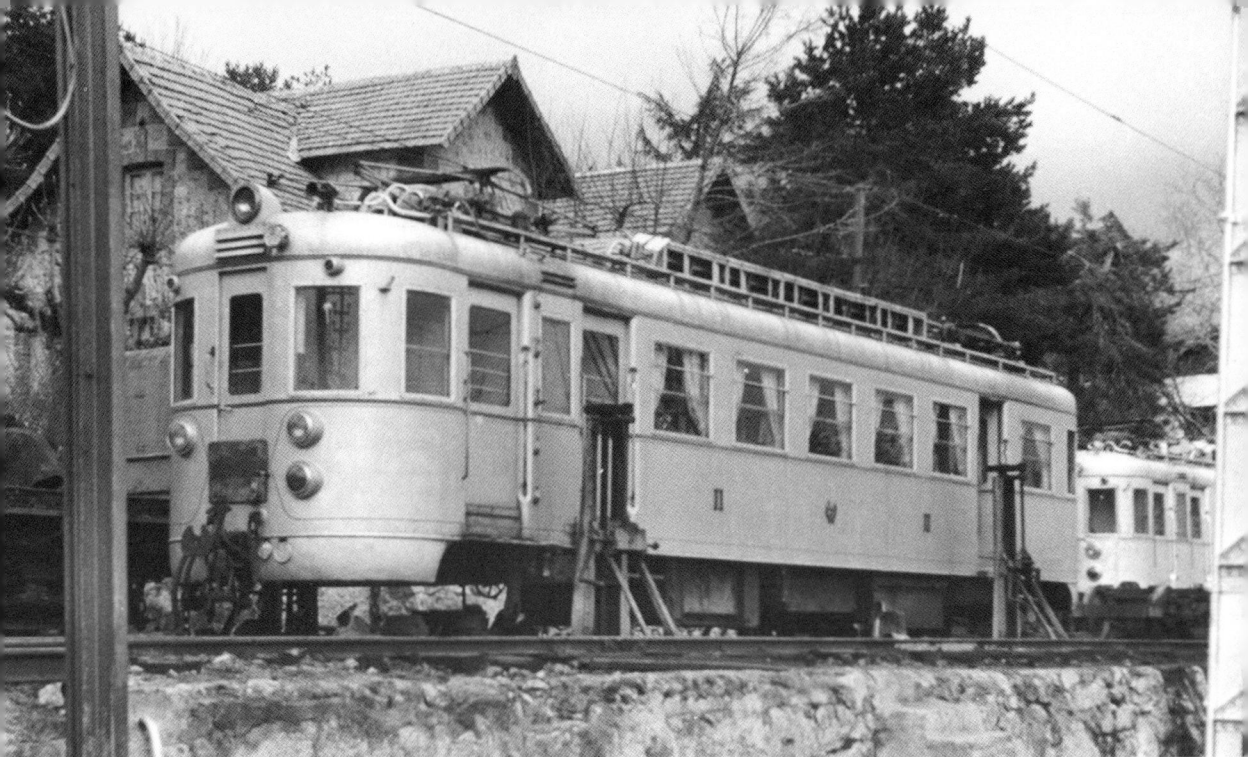

2.15.   One of the short lived SECN units was viewed at Cercedilla whilst undergoing maintenance to its bogies on 1st April 1966. (J.Wiseman)

2.16.   A recently supplied RENFE diesel locomotive was recorded at Cercedilla on the same occasion. This machine would normally be used for shunting operations and track maintenance work when the electric power supply was switched off. Note the Swiss built snowplough attached to the locomotive. (J.Wiseman)

2.17.   Two of the Swiss units, nos WM101 and WM103, were witnessed as they headed north at Navacerrada, bound for Los Cotos, on 1st April 1966. (J.Wiseman)

2.18.   One of the later MTM units was photographed on the final descent to Cercedilla, shortly after entering service, on 27th July 1976. (J.Wiseman)

2.19   A four car MTM unit was viewed at a snow covered Cercedilla, prior to departure to Los Cotos on 8th December 1990. (D.Trevor Rowe)

2.20.　Upon arrival at Los Cotos, the MTM multiple unit has allowed its payload of ski enthusiasts to disembark, prior to returning to the lower terminus. (D.Trevor Rowe)

3. Valdepeñas to Peñarroya

Situated about 200km south of Madrid is the industrial town of Puertollano, which lies in a saddle between two ranges of barren hills that resemble the surface of the Moon. More relevant for this publication is the fact that two very contrasting narrow gauge railways terminated at this location. In addition, Puertollano is also served by a RENFE broad gauge route that runs from Madrid to Seville and the southern coast. The two narrow gauge lines were unconnected and of different gauges. They were completely different in character and served the contrasting needs of the regions through which they operated.

V.   The hinterland of Southern Spain once boasted a large number of narrow gauge railways which served the principal towns and cities in the area. All are shown on this diagram, which depicts the routes at their greatest extent. The Huelva enlargement appears at the beginning of section 5, opposite photograph 5.1. (D.H.Smith)

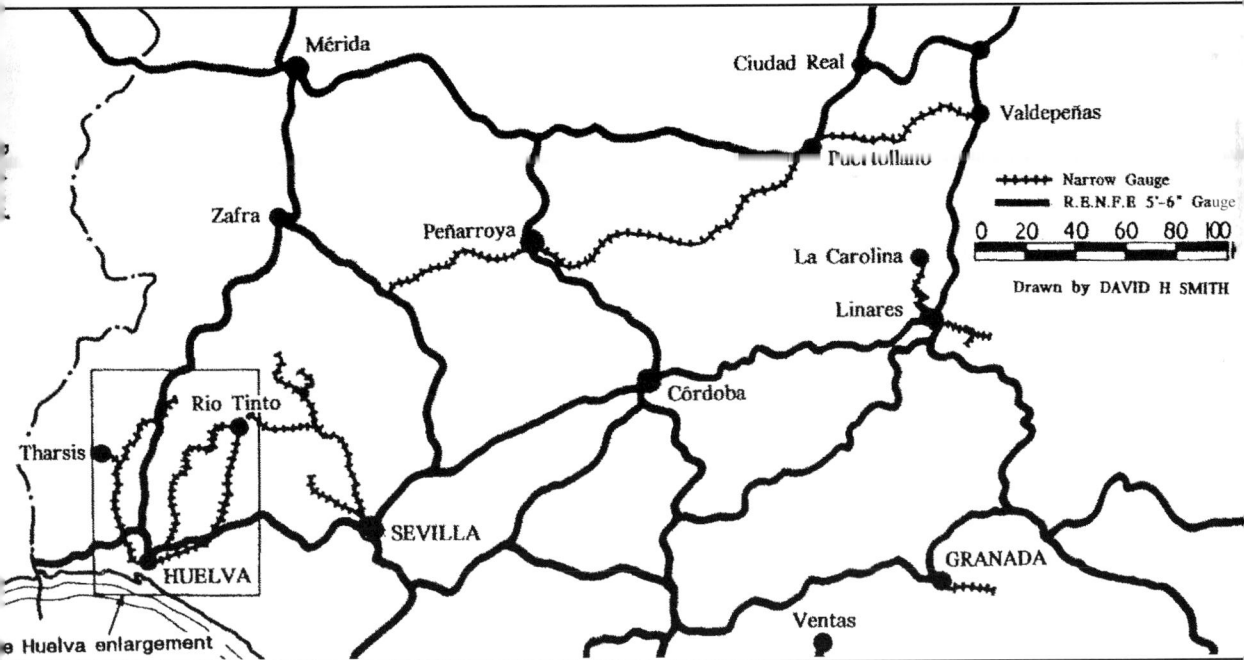

VALDEPEÑAS - PUERTOLLANO

The Ferrocarril de Valdepeñas a Puertollano was a 750mm gauge railway, 76km in length, which was constructed to serve the wine producing and agricultural region centred near Valdepeñas. Opened in 1891, the company operated a typically rural railway passing through delightful countryside to the north-east of Puertollano. Unlike many of its contemporaries, passengers were considered to be more important than the transport of freight. Being an agricultural area, the latter consisted mainly of the produce of the region, much of which was transported in mixed trains.

Originally an independent company, the line was taken over by ESTADO during the 1940s although the operation hardly changed following their involvement. Sadly this most attractive railway eventually succumbed to the "march of progress" and was closed in 1963. During the final decade of operation, two trains per day in each direction were deemed sufficient to maintain the service.

During the 72 year life of the line, the motive power consisted of six small locomotives, which survived until closure. These consisted of three Couillet 0-6-0s which were originally supplied as 0-6-0Ts for the opening of the line in 1891, being converted to tender engines early in their lives. These were joined in 1903 by two Jung 0-4-2s and an Orenstein & Koppel 0-6-0. This was to be the total fleet until 1956 when three O&K 0-4-0Ts were transferred by ESTADO from the recently closed FC de Flassá a Palamós, Gerona y Bañolas in Catalonia. Some additional carriages from the same source also joined the stock at that time.

3.1.   Couillet 0-6-0 no.3 *Belgica* was witnessed outside the depot at Valdepeñas on 3rd April 1961. Originally constructed as a 0-6-0T in 1894, it was converted and gained a tender early in its life. (J.Wiseman)

3.2.	A selection of the passenger rolling stock was recorded on the same occasion. The bogie carriage was one of those transferred from Catalonia in 1956. (J.Wiseman)

3.3.	O & K 0-6-0 no.6 *Asturias* was being prepared for service when it was photographed at Valdepeñas depot on 22nd April 1962. (D. Trevor Rowe)

3.4.   This more detailed view of the O & K 0-6-0 clearly shows the small tender, which was almost certainly constructed locally along with those for the earlier Couillet locomotives. (D.Trevor Rowe)

3.5.   O & K 0-6-0 no.6 was recorded at Valdepeñas, prior to departing with a passenger train bound for Puertollano on 22nd April 1962. (D.Trevor Rowe)

3.6.   No.6 was also on passenger train duty when it was viewed at La Zarza with a Puertollano bound train on 20th May 1962. (L.G.Marshall)

3.7. Couillet no.3 was engaged in some shunting at Calzada during the course of its journey from Puertollano on 22nd April 1962. (D.Trevor Rowe)

3.8. With the shunting completed, no.3 received the attention of an oilcan before continuing its journey to the eastern terminus. (D.Trevor Rowe)

3.9. On the other side of the station, O & K no.6 was recorded as it departed towards Puertollano on the same occasion. (D.Trevor Rowe)

3.10. The mid point station at Calzada is featured in this view of Couillet 0-6-0 no.1 *Vitoria* on 20th May 1962. (L.G.Marshall)

3.11.   Viewed standing astride a 750mm gauge level crossing, this picture of no.1 illustrates another of the Spanish built tenders attached to these Belgian locomotives early in their lives. (L.G.Marshall)

3.12.   O & K no.6 was recorded traversing the grass strewn track near Calzada during the course of a journey to Puertollano on 22nd April 1962. (D.Trevor Rowe)

3.13.   The flat plains near the western end of the line provided the backdrop for this view of no.6 on the same occasion. (D.Trevor Rowe)

3.14.   With a barren hillside dominating the scene, no.6 was recorded as it arrived at Puertollano on the completion of its 76km long journey from Valdepeñas on 22nd April 1962. (D.Trevor Rowe)

3.15.   A short time later, the O & K 0-6-0 drew to a halt at the station, prior to shunting the stock into the sidings. (D.Trevor Rowe)

PUERTOLLANO - PEÑARROYA

By complete contrast to the 750mm gauge railway, the other narrow gauge line serving Puertollano was a metre gauge route 218km in length. The FC Puertollano y Peñarroya (PP), which actually terminated at Fuente del Arco to the west of Peñarroya, was principally a freight carrying line serving the extensive mining activities that operated in this arid and inhospitable region.

Completed in 1881, the railway was built and operated by a French company the Sociedad Minera y Metalúrgica de Peñarroya (SMMP), with the result that much of the equipment was of French origin. In addition to the extensive metre gauge system, the SMMP also operated a broad gauge branch which connected with the RENFE at Peñarroya. There was also a connection with the broad gauge system of the ENCAR coal mines at the same location, whilst at Mina Asdrubal the SMMP also ran a small 640mm gauge line.

Due to the extensive amount of freight traffic working along the heavily graded route, the 50km long section with the steepest gradients between Puertollano and Conquista was electrified at 3000vDC in 1927. During the 1950s, the operation of the line was passed to ESTADO and subsequently FEVE, who introduced Billard railcars for the limited passenger services on offer. The narrow gauge sections of the system finally closed in 1970, although some of the broad gauge connections to the RENFE network remained in use after that time.

Initially a quartet of Fives-Lille 0-6-0Ts were supplied which were joined between 1896 and 1907 by fourteen 0-8-0Ts from Fives-Lille and SACM. The latter concern also supplied three 4-6-0Ts in 1914 whilst in addition there was a La Meuse 2-8-0T and a Henschel 0-6-6-0T Mallet. Finally, in 1953 a trio of Franco-Belge 2-10-0s dating from 1931 was acquired from Tunisia, these being joined by two former Swiss Rhätische Bahn SLM 2-4-4-0T Mallets which were transferred from the Catalan system in 1964.The electrified section was operated by five French built B-B machines, which looked like scaled down SNCF locomotives of the period.

3.16. Following the electrification of the eastern section of the PP route in 1927, five large B-B locomotives built in France provided the motive power. No.101 was recorded at Puertollano whilst shunting stock on 23rd April 1962. (D.Trevor Rowe)

3.17.   Billard railcars were introduced by ESTADO during the 1950s in an attempt to re-invigorate the passenger services. Unit no.2130 was photographed at Almodóvar, the midway point of the route, on the same date. (D.Trevor Rowe)

3.18.   Fives-Lille 0-6-0T no.1 *Almodovar del Campo* was witnessed amid the extensive complex at Peñarroya, whilst its rake of wagons and vans were being loaded on 20th September 1963. (D. Trevor Rowe)

3.19.   SACM 0-8-0T no.8 *Peñarroya* was viewed inside the depot at Peñarroya, whilst awaiting its next turn of duty, on 4th April 1961. (J.Wiseman)

3.20.   Two of the SACM 4-6-0Ts, with no.20 to the fore, were recorded at the depot on 24th April 1962. The majority of the PP locomotives bore names, this example rejoicing in the grand title of *Pueblonuevo del Terrible*. (D.Trevor Rowe)

3.21.   Fives Lille 0-8-0T no.12 *Alcaracejos* was positioned on the traverser at Peñarroya depot when it was photographed on 23rd April 1962. (D.Trevor Rowe)

3.22.   No.23, the Henschel 0-6-6-0T Mallet of 1917 vintage, was witnessed at the depot on the same occasion. The length of this large locomotive can be appreciated in this view, whilst one of the smaller machines is almost dwarfed alongside. (D.Trevor Rowe)

3.23.   SACM 4-6-0T no.21 *Fuente del Arco* was minus its dome cover when it was recorded at the depot on 29th March 1966. (L.G.Marshall)

3.24.   Fives-Lille 0-8-0T no.10 *Belmez* was in the process of shunting no.21 (seen in picture 3.23) when viewed on the same occasion. (L.G.Marshall)

3.25.   4-6-0T no.21 was hauling a mixed train from Fuente de Arco when it was photographed approaching Peñarroya on 4th April 1961. (J.Wiseman)

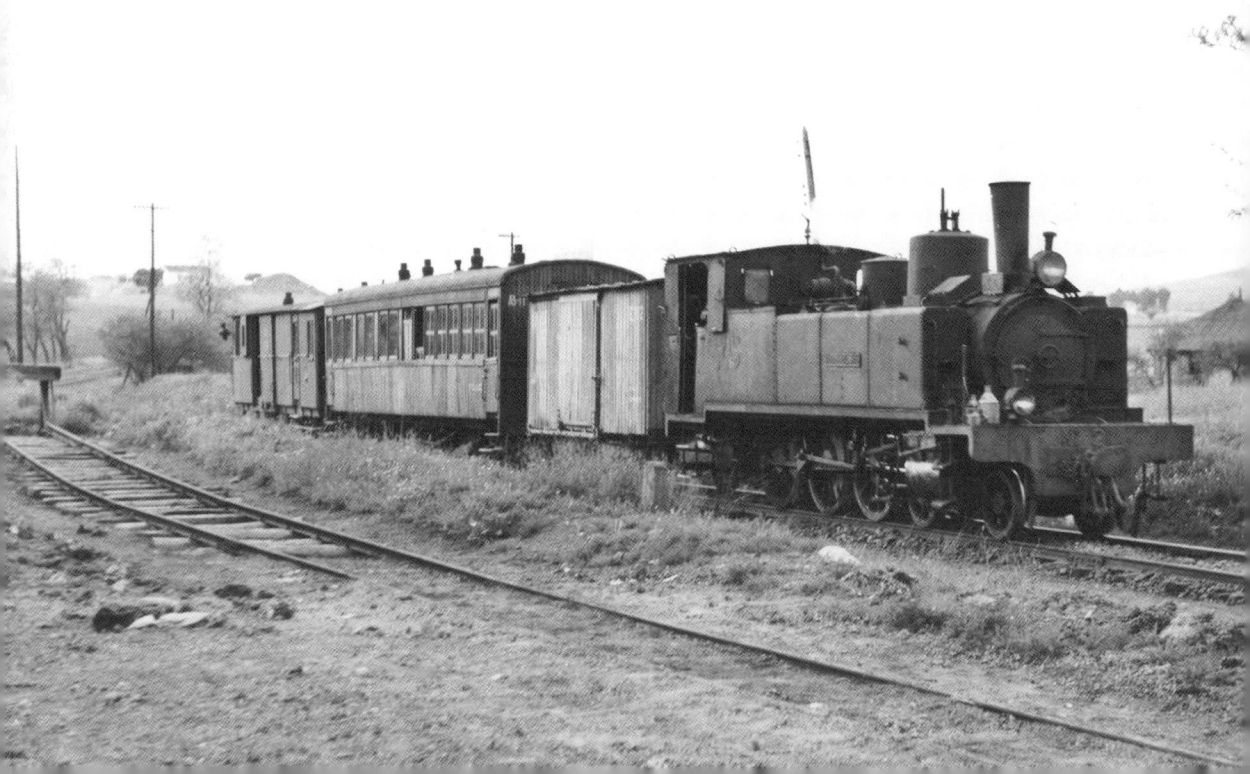

3.26.   Fives-Lille 0-6-0T no.4 *Puertollano* was in service at the SMMP works at Mina Asdrubal when it was witnessed on 23rd April 1962. (D.Trevor Rowe)

3.27.   SMMP also had a 640mm gauge system at the works complex. Couillet 0-4-0T no.2 was resting in its shed at Mina Asdrubal, when viewed on the same date. (D.Trevor Rowe)

3.28.   On the SMMP broad gauge connection to the RENFE network, a Couillet 0-6-0T was recorded at the head of a long rake of empty wagons in the transfer sidings at Peñarroya on 19th September 1963. (D.Trevor Rowe)

4. Linares, Granada and Seville

We now enter the ancient realm of Andalucia, which embraces much of the Southern part of Spain. To the east of the region were three relatively small narrow gauge operations situated around Linares and Granada, whilst further west two important metre gauge mineral lines were to be found near Seville. The latter terminated close to the extensive mining regions of Huelva and provided an alternative supply route from the mines to the RENFE network serving the hinterland.

LINARES - LA CAROLINA

Situated to the south of Puertollano is the town of Linares, which is located in an area notable for its lead mines. In order to serve the mines and provide access to the main line system, the Ferrocarril de La Carolina y Prolongaciones (CP) was opened in 1908. This 39km long metre gauge route was principally built to serve the lead mines but also provided a passenger service. This was not a particularly rapid service, the twice daily mixed train requiring over two hours with much shunting required during the course of the journey. Passenger traffic dwindled in favour of road transport during the 1950s, whilst the mine's output ultimately followed suit. As a consequence the line closed in 1961.

During the 53 year life of the CP, four 0-8-0Ts supplied by St. Leonard, Liege, provided all the motive power. These hauled an assorted collection of rolling stock through this arid region of southern Spain, running north to La Carolina.

4.1.   CP 0-8-0T no.2 *Linares* was recorded at the head of empty wagons amid the decaying remnants of the Linares station complex on 12th October 1959. (J.Wiseman)

4.2.   Following the closure of the CP, 0-8-0T no.4 *San Roque* was still residing in the roofless depot at Linares when it was photographed on 22nd April 1962. (D.Trevor Rowe)

LINARES TRAMWAY SYSTEM

In addition to the steam operated line, Linares was also served by an extensive metre gauge 600v DC electric tramway system. The FC Eléctrico de la Loma initially opened in 1907 with a 23km long line which connected the Linares town tramway system at Baeza-Empalme, on the main line between Madrid and Granada, to Ubeda. In 1914 a 6.5km long line was opened from Baeza to connect with the CP, whilst a 5km branch was also installed to serve La Yedra.

This basically roadside tramway was taken over by ESTADO in 1936 and by the early 1950s was in a very decrepit condition with the original tramcars still in service. In 1953 work began on modernizing the system which would have resulted in a 1500v DC light railway running on its own right of way. A completely new station at Ubeda was completed in 1962, although devoid of tracks, and new trainsets were ordered. However the work was halted in 1964 and the complete system was closed in 1966.

4.3.	On the town section of the Linares Tramway System, car no.8 was viewed as it traversed the main street of Linares on 22nd April 1962. (D.Trevor Rowe)

4.4.	Car no.17 was witnessed as it shunted a van across a level crossing at Ubeda on 21st April 1962, whilst the local residents continue with their daily business amid the activity. (D.Trevor Rowe)

4.5.   Electric locomotive no.L22 and trailer car no.28 were stabled at Ubeda depot when they were photographed on the same occasion. (D.Trevor Rowe)

4.6.   Car no.14 was recorded at Baeza with a service providing a connection with the RENFE station at Empalme on 21st April 1962. (D.Trevor Rowe)

4.7.   Witnessed to the west of the interchange station at Baeza Empalme, car no.10 was towing an overhead wire maintenance tower whilst a length of rail was attached to the side of the vehicle. This interesting scene was recorded on 10th April 1963. (J.Wiseman)

4.8.   At San Roque, where the electric line formerly connected with the steam operated CP, car no. 8 was photographed as it departed with a service bound for Baeza on 10th April 1963. (J. Wiseman)

GRANADA - SIERRA NEVADA

        Another city with an extensive tramway system was Granada. This metre gauge network had been in operation from the early years of the 20th century. However in 1925 it was connected to a 750mm gauge 600v DC light railway known as the Granada-Sierra Nevada line. Opened in 1925 from Granada to Maitena, the line was taken over by ESTADO in 1931. It was ultimately extended to San Juan in 1950, in order to serve the developing winter sports centres. The 21km long route passed through some dramatic and rugged scenery, with the fleet of four tramcars maintaining the service throughout the entire life of the line. Despite extensions to serve the additional ski resorts being planned, this interesting line succumbed to closure in 1974.

4.9.   Sierra Nevada car no. 4 was recorded at Pinos Genil whilst en route from Granada to San Juan on 8th April 1956. (D.Trevor Rowe)

4.10.   At the original terminus at Maitena, car no.1 was operating another service bound for San Juan on the same occasion. (D.Trevor Rowe)

4.11.   The Sierra Nevada line traversed some spectacular scenery during the course of its 21km length, as seen by this view from the tram driving compartment of the bridge across the Río Genil on 8th April 1956. (D.Trevor Rowe)

SEVILLE - CALA MINES

On the northern outskirts of the historic city of Seville was the southern terminus of an extensive metre gauge industrial network. The 97km long Minas de Cala line served the mines which were situated on the eastern extremity of the extensive mining area of Huelva. The headquarters of the line were situated at San Juan de Aznalfarache, alongside the Río Guadalquivir and also served by the Seville tramway system. Opened in 1904, the line provided a passenger service until 1938. However it was the minerals which provided the majority of the traffic, until the 1950s when other forms of transport were deemed to be more efficient and the line eventually closed by the end of the decade. To operate the steeply graded line, seven powerful 0-6-4Ts where supplied by Borsig in 1904 along with three 0-4-0Ts from the same manufacturer between 1906 and 1911 for lighter duties.

4.12.   At the depot of the Cala Mines line at San Juan de Aznalfarache, Borsig 0-4-0Ts nos.34 *Barrenra* (front) and 33 *Guadalquivír* were positioned on the shed road whilst a trio of Borsig 0-6-4Ts stood alongside the shed on 27th April 1962. (D.Trevor Rowe)

4.13.   The rear locomotive in the line of 0-6-4Ts was no.1 *Conde de Rodas*, which was stabled alongside some very weary looking rolling stock amid the grass strewn sidings. (D.Trevor Rowe)

4.14.   This broadside view of 0-6-4T no.3, named *Zufre*, exemplifies the massive proportions of these Borsig locomotives. (D.Trevor Rowe)

CAMAS - AZNALCÓLLAR

Situated near to the terminus of the Cala Mines line was the terminus of the FC Aznalcóllar al Guadalquivir (FCAG) at Camas. In order to reach their respective depots, the two lines crossed each other near Camas. The 48km long metre gauge line commenced operation in 1908 and ran in a westerly direction, serving the pyrites mines at Aznalcóllar. This line also succumbed to closure before 1960, although during the following decade the dual gauge connection between Camas and the riverside wharfs remained in use. During this period, metre gauge locomotives were often seen hauling broad gauge wagons. The locomotive fleet consisted of six 0-6-2Ts from Jung and Krauss supplied in 1908, whilst a Fives-Lille 0-8-0T was transferred from the Peñarroya-Puertollano line in 1956.

4.15. At Camas depot of the FCAG, Krauss 0-6-2T no.5 was recorded whilst between duties on 10th April 1964. This attractive locomotive was named *Triana*. (J.Wiseman)

4.16. During the final period of operation, no. 5 was also in action between Camas and the riverside wharfs when it was photographed during shunting operations on 31st March 1966. (L.G.Marshall)

5. The Mineral Wealth of Huelva

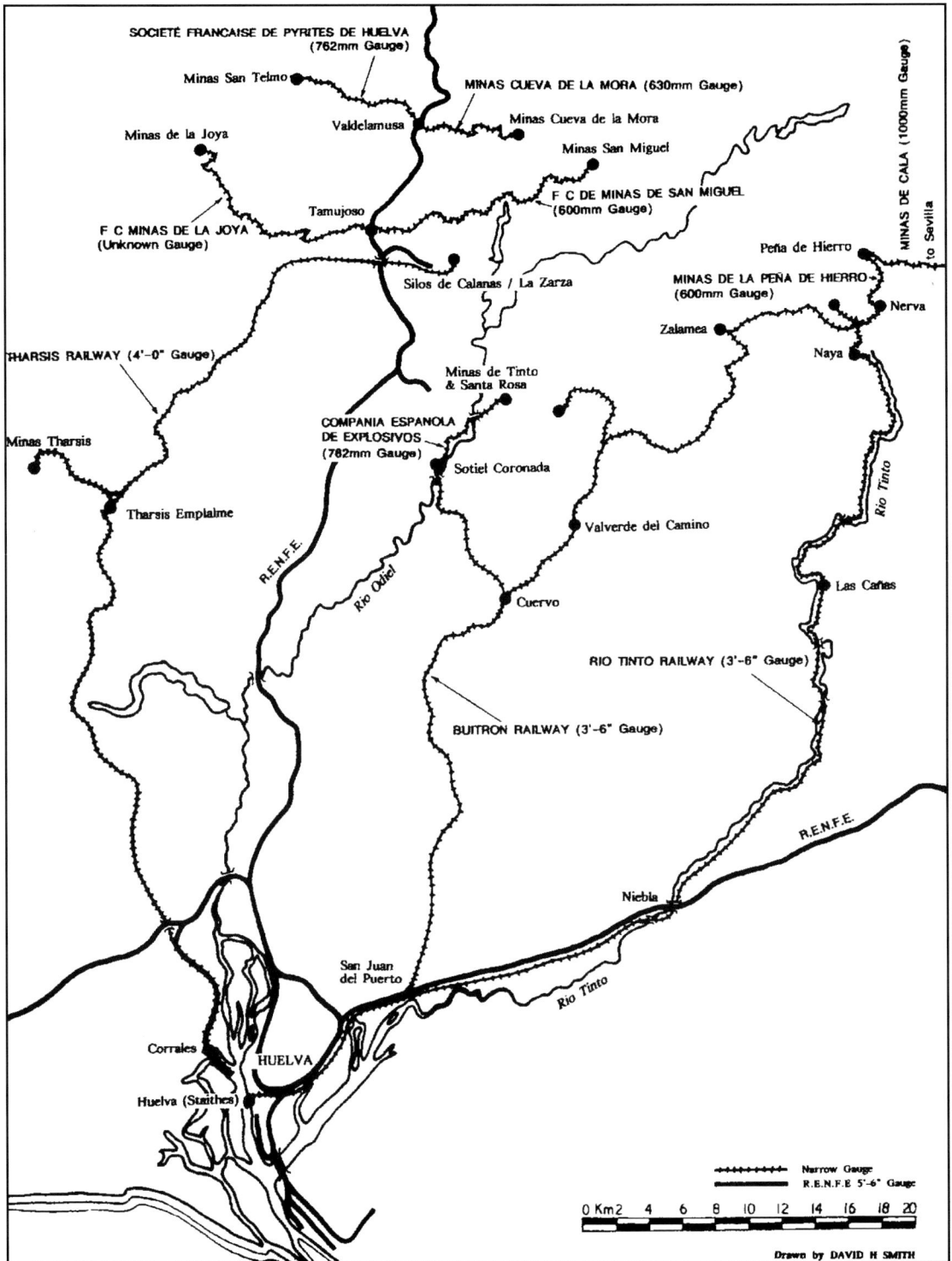

SOCIETÉ FRANCAISE DE PYRITES DE HUELVA
(762mm Gauge)

Minas San Telmo

MINAS CUEVA DE LA MORA (630mm Gauge)

Minas de la Joya

Valdelamusa

Minas Cueva de la Mora

Minas San Miguel

F C MINAS DE LA JOYA
(Unknown Gauge)

Tamujoso

F C DE MINAS DE SAN MIGUEL
(600mm Gauge)

MINAS DE CALA (1000mm Gauge)

to Sevilla

Peña de Hierro

Silos de Calanas / La Zarza

MINAS DE LA PEÑA DE HIERRO
(600mm Gauge)

Nerva

THARSIS RAILWAY (4'-0" Gauge)

Zalamea

Naya

Minas Tharsis

Minas de Tinto
& Santa Rosa

COMPANIA ESPANOLA
DE EXPLOSIVOS
(782mm Gauge)

Tharsis Emplalme

Sotiel Coronada

Valverde del Camino

Rio Tinto

Las Cañas

R.E.N.F.E.

Rio Odiel

Cuervo

RIO TINTO RAILWAY (3'-6" Gauge)

BUITRON RAILWAY (3'-6" Gauge)

R.E.N.F.E.

Niebla

San Juan
del Puerto

Rio Tinto

Corrales

HUELVA

Huelva (Staithes)

Narrow Gauge

R.E.N.F.E 5'-6" Gauge

0 Km 2   4   6   8   10   12   14   16   18   20

Drawn by DAVID H SMITH

Located to the west of Andalucia is the province of Huelva which also embraces the coastal region along the Gulf of Cadiz. The hinterland of Huelva was dominated by a vast region of barren mountainous country rich in minerals, which have been exploited since prehistoric times. Over 3000 years ago gold and silver was extracted whilst the Romans were mining copper a millennium later. However it was the presence of huge deposits of iron pyrites which attracted the attention of industrialists during the 19th century and the construction of three extensive narrow gauge railways to transport the ore to the coastal ports. The three lines were all of British origin with equipment from the same source as a result of the exploitation of the pyrites by British owned companies. In addition to the principal railways, a number of smaller lines were established around the mining areas which acted as feeders to the main systems. Among these smaller operations were the grandly named French owned 762mm gauge Société Française des Pyrites de Huelva (SFPH) in the north of the area, whilst another 762mm gauge line was the Compañía Española de Explosivos (CEE) located at Sotiel Coranando in the centre of the mining region. Both of these short lines closed during the early 1960s although reminders of their past exploits remained on site for a few more years.

← VI. The vast network of railways serving the Huelva mining operations are shown prior to the 1960s. (D.H.Smith)

5.1.   During the final months of the 762mm gauge SFPH operation, Hartmann 0-6-0T no.6 was looking somewhat forlorn amid scenes of abandonment at San Telmo depot on 22nd September 1963. (D.Trevor Rowe)

5.2.   Scenes of dereliction surrounded this Bagnal 0-4-0ST when it was photographed at Sotiel Coranando on 26th April 1962, at around the time the CEE closed. (D.Trevor Rowe)

RÍO TINTO RAILWAY

Formed in 1871 by a group of British financiers, the Río Tinto Company obtained the rights to mine the pyrites in the area to the north of Huelva. Although a large sum was paid to the Spanish government for these rights, it was ultimately to become a major source of friction between the two governments. However this friction was far in the future when the 1067mm (3ft 6in) gauge railway was opened in 1875 to link the mines at Río Tinto with the extensive port at Huelva, a distance of 83km. Although principally a mineral railway, a limited passenger service was also provided. Originally for the use of the mine workers, who were allowed free travel, the line ultimately operated a public service for the benefit of the many villages along the route. From the extensive squalid mining surroundings which were also served by an internal system, much of it underground, the main line passed across the barren wasteland before descending through a deep gorge shared with the river. Numerous tunnels and bridges were encountered along this dramatic section of railway before the line emerged onto the coastal plain. An extensive complex was developed at Huelva where in addition to the warehouses and staithes of the port, transhipment sidings alongside the RENFE broad gauge route were also installed.

In addition to the British motive power and rolling stock, the railway was fully signalled with a huge array of equipment that would have looked equally at home in the mining areas of County Durham and South Wales. Likewise the architecture of the railway infrastructure had a definite British appearance, despite being located in an area far different in its scenic attributes. The locomotive fleet comprised of a large number of machines, 248 being supplied in total throughout the life of the railway – of which over 120 were in use during the peak periods of operation. The majority were 0-6-0Ts supplied in various batches between 1874 and 1912 from sources such as Beyer Peacock, Dübs, North British and Avonside. The major exceptions were six 0-8-0Ts from Baldwin in 1901 and four 0-6-0Ts from the same manufacturer in 1907. Beyer Peacock also supplied two 2-6-2+2-6-2 Garratts in 1929 whilst the final additions to the fleet were six powerful 2-6-0s from Robert Stephenson & Hawthorns in 1953/4. Diesel locomotives also appeared on the scene during the 1960s and 70s, mainly of Spanish or American construction. The passenger carriages were mainly the products of the Gloucester or Birmingham Carriage & Wagon Companies. The latter supplied a sumptuous bogie vehicle known as "The Maharajah's Saloon" for use by the directors and visiting VIPs, this being from a cancelled order destined for India.

In 1954 the company was sold to a Spanish consortium, which initially continued to operate the railway and mines in much the same way as its predecessors. However with a contraction of traditional mining methods during the following two decades, the railway operation declined, with the passenger service ending in 1971 and a total closure in 1984.

Since that date, eleven locomotives and a number of items of rolling stock survived in order to provide the basis for a museum at the mines devoted to the history of the line and its associated mining industry. In conjunction with this, a 14km stretch of the upper section of the route from the mines to the gorge has been retained for occasional special workings. Due to the fire risk, diesel power is normally used for the journey through the gorge, although steam locomotives are allowed to operate at the former mining complex.

5.3.   This panoramic view of the mining complex at Río Tinto from April 1962 clearly shows the extent of the operation. The large building in the centre of the illustration is the locomotive depot and workshops, whilst in the foreground can be seen some of the houses of the mining village. (D.Trevor Rowe)

5.4.   The railway was fully signalled, as exemplified by this large gantry at Río Tinto Estacion. A rake of workman's carriages can be seen on the far side of the platform in this view recorded on 22nd September 1963. (D.Trevor Rowe)

5.5.   Dübs I-class 0-6-0T no.77 was witnessed as it departed from Río Tinto with a load of hopper wagons bound for Huelva on 25th March 1961. (L.G.Marshall)

5.6.   Beyer Peacock C-class 0-6-0T no.13 was coupled to an improvised tender when it was viewed alongside the locomotive depot on 24th March 1961. (L.G. Marshall)

5.7.   A load of empty wagons hauled by North British K-class 0-6-0T no.106 was recorded on one of the mines branches at Río Tinto 26th April 1962. (D.Trevor Rowe)

5.8.   Two of the North British K-class 0-6-0Ts, nos 133 and 103, were stabled outside the depot when they were photographed on 26th April 1962. (D.Trevor Rowe)

5.9.   Dübs I-class 0-6-0T no.49 of 1881 vintage was in steam outside the depot when it was viewed on 22nd September 1963. (D.Trevor Rowe)

5.10.   No.109, one of the later North British K-class 0-6-0Ts supplied in 1907, was resting between duties outside Río Tinto depot when witnessed on 26th April 1962. (D.Trevor Rowe)

5.11.   On the same occasion no.201, one of the impressive 2-6-0s supplied in 1953 by Robert Stephenson & Hawthorns, was being prepared for service outside the depot. The crew obviously relished the thought of being photographed! (D.Trevor Rowe)

5.12.   K-class no.118 was fitted with a larger bunker and converted to a 0-6-2T in an attempt to increase its operational capabilities. The modified locomotive was recorded alongside the boiler unit of Beyer-Garratt no.145 at Río Tinto depot on 22nd January 1965. (J.Wiseman)

5.13. 2-6-0 no. 201 was witnessed as it passed through Río Tinto Estacion, en route to the depot, on the same occasion. (J.Wiseman)

5.14. Fitted with a coal hopper above the bunker, Dübs I-class 0-6-0T no.51 was being prepared for duty when it was viewed on 1st June 1970. (L.G.Marshall)

5.15.   Hawthorn Leslie supplied two 0-4-0 crane tanks; one in 1913 and another in 1930. No.150, the later of the pair, was photographed outside the depot alongside North British 0-6-0T no.86 on 1st June 1970. (L.G.Marshall)

5.16.   On the Zalamea branch line at El Valle, a workman's train hauled by Beyer Peacock C-class 0-6-0T no.13 was recorded whilst en-route to Río Tinto on 22nd January 1965. (J.Wiseman)

5.17.   Deep in the gorge at Las Cañas, Beyer-Garratt no.146 had paused in the passing loop whilst hauling a loaded train for Huelva on 24th March 1961. (L.G.Marshall)

5.18.   Near the southern end of the main line at Las Mallas, 2-6-0 no.201 was in charge of a heavy load of pyrites bound for Huelva when it was photographed receiving some attention to its bogie wheel set on 2nd June 1970. (L.G.Marshall)

5.19.   In contrast to the barren landscape at the mines complex, the depot at Huelva was set amid far greener surroundings. Dübs I-class 0-6-0T no.73 was at rest near the depot on 24th September 1963. (D.Trevor Rowe)

5.20.   The first of the 2-6-0s supplied in 1953, no.200, is seen as it was raising steam at Huelva on 2nd June 1970. (L.G.Marshall)

5.21.   2-6-0 no.202 was recorded as it made a spirited departure from Huelva with a load of empty hopper wagons bound for Río Tinto on the same date. (L.G.Marshall)

BUITRÓN RAILWAY

A short distance to the northeast of Huelva at San Juan del Puerto, another 1067mm gauge railway connected with the Río Tinto system. Running in a northerly direction, the 36km long Buitrón-San Juan de Puerto Railway in fact pre-dated its larger neighbour, having commenced operations in 1868 for freight and a limited passenger service in 1874. Owned and constructed by the United Alkali Company, its main purpose was the transport of pyrites from the company's mines near Buitrón, a 99 year concession having been obtained from the Spanish government. In 1926 the company was taken over by Imperial Chemical Industries (ICI), thus continuing the British connection. Unfortunately the takeover by ICI was at a time when the mines were showing a definite decrease in production.

In addition the passenger service, which had always been poorly supported, was faltering to the extent that it ceased to operate after 1934. ICI sold the mines complex in 1941 whilst the railway was taken over by ESTADO. The latter attempted to reinvigorate the railway with a resumption of passenger services during the 1940s, railcars being introduced for the three daily services during the 1960s. Some of these services connected with the Río Tinto line at Zalamea, which allowed some additional flexibility to the operation. However with the continuing contraction of the mining activities and the subsequent lack of passengers, ESTADO closed the line in 1968.

The principal locomotive fleet consisted of 0-6-0Ts and 4-6-0Ts supplied by Kitson and Andrew Barclay between 1868 and 1908, all of which carried names relating to the area served by the railway. ESTADO introduced some of their familiar Billard railcars during the final years of operation in an attempt to improve the passenger service, whilst the remaining steam locomotives were gradually withdrawn from service.

5.22.   An ESTADO Billard railcar is viewed in the Buitrón bay platform at San Juan de Puerto, whilst alongside a RENFE 4-6-0 no.231-2013 awaits departure with a train from Seville to Huelva, on 25th March 1961. (L.G.Marshall)

5.23.   The first locomotive supplied to the Buitrón railway was this Kitson 0-4-0T supplied in 1868. Named *Victoria*, no.1 was recorded on the upper reaches of the line at Valverde de Camino on 25th March 1961. (L.G.Marshall)

5.24.   Minus its side tanks, Kitson 0-6-0T no.12 *Concepción* was receiving attention in the depot at Valverde when it was viewed on 21st January 1965. (J.Wiseman)

5.25.   The line featured an inclined plane, known as "La Fija", near Zalamea at the northern end of the route. Borsig 0-4-0T no.19 *El Rella* was photographed at the top of the incline, where it was used as the top shunter, on 22nd January 1965. (J.Wiseman)

THARSIS RAILWAY

The third of the principal narrow gauge railways in the Huelva region was located a short distance to the west of its neighbours and differed in one important respect. A Glasgow based company known as The Tharsis Copper and Sulphur Company obtained a concession in 1866 to construct a railway from its mines at Tharsis to the coast at Puntal de la Cruz. The 75km long line was constructed to the relatively unusual gauge of 1219mm (4ft 0in), the reasons for this choice being lost in time. The fact that the Glasgow underground system adopted this gauge may have some tenuous bearing on the unusual choice.

For over a century, the Tharsis Company operated a comprehensive service, principally transporting ore from the various mines served by the line. A limited passenger service using the original four wheeled carriages was also provided, although by the later years of the operation this had been reduced to a once weekly train over the southern section of the route on the coastal plain. Freight loadings were equally as heavy as those on the Río Tinto line, whilst the port at Puntal de la Cruz was a substantial operation in its own right. The latter was situated on the opposite bank of the Río Odiel to the corresponding port at Huelva, both of which were among the major employers of this coastal region.

To operate this long and well organized railway, the Tharsis line adopted a standard range of powerful locomotives. Initially modest 0-4-0Ts from Dübs were provided in 1867, being joined by North British 0-6-0Ts and 0-8-0Ts between 1904 and 1915. By 1923 traffic had increased to such an extent that more powerful motive power was required. This resulted in a fleet of seven Hohenzollern 2-8-0Ts supplied between 1923 and 1930, the final example being constructed by Krupp. These German built locomotives were joined in 1930 by an additional four 2-8-0Ts from North British, whilst between 1950 and 1955 the Glasgow manufacturer supplied another eight 0-8-0Ts. During the final years of the operation, six Alstom Bo-Bo diesel locomotives were added to the fleet. However it was the large and powerful German and Scottish 2-8-0Ts that were indelibly associated with the line during the heyday of its operation. All the steam locomotives bore names associated with the area served by the line.

Despite outliving its neighbouring railways, the Tharsis operation ultimately suffered from the contraction of the mining industry and competition from road transport for what little traffic remained. As a consequence, the railway closed in 1999. However a newly formed Spanish company has recently obtained the rights for an opencast mining operation in the area. Whilst this new development is welcome news for the economy of the area, it is doubtful if the railway will benefit from it operation. However the surviving Alstom diesel locomotives were still stored in the former depot at Tharsis ten years after the closure of the line.

5.26. The principal locomotive depot of the Tharsis line was situated at Corrales, near Puntal de la Cruz. The pioneer Dübs 0-4-0T no.1, *Odiel* of 1867 was recorded at the depot on 23rd September 1963. (D.Trevor Rowe)

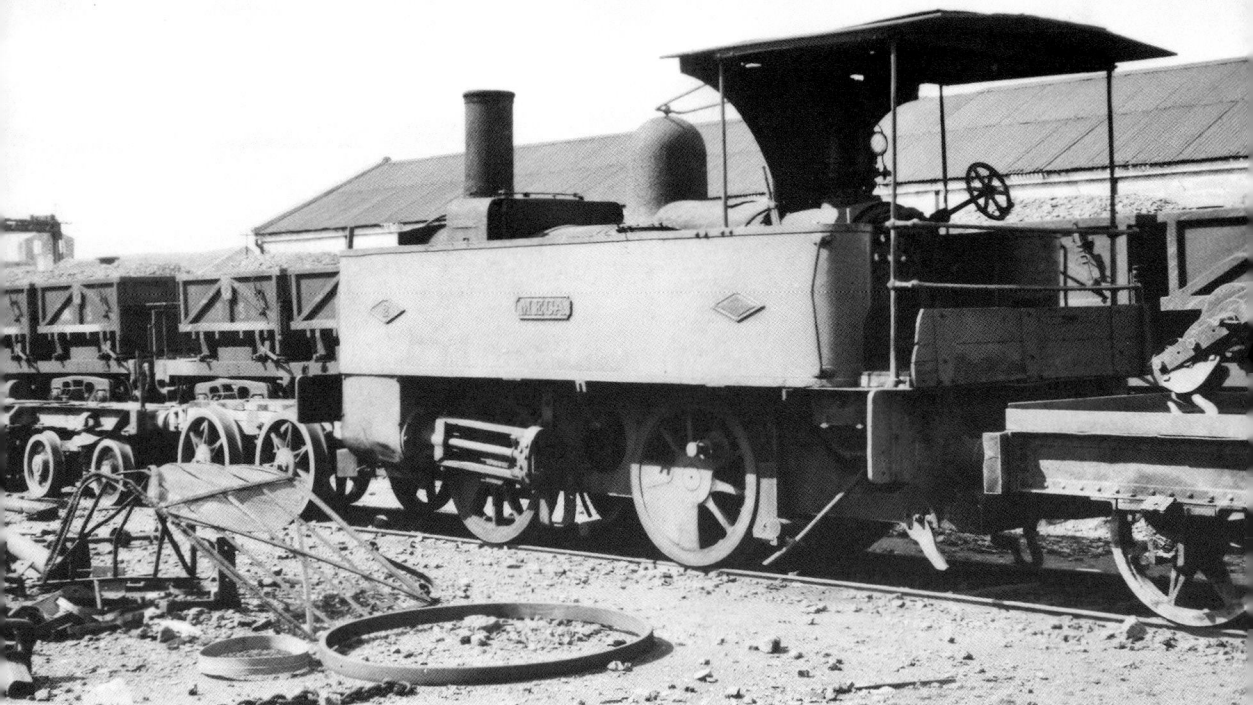

5.27.   Sister locomotive no.2 *Meca* was looking somewhat incomplete when it was viewed among an assortment of rolling stock on 25th April 1962. (D.Trevor Rowe)

5.28.   One of the four wheeled carriages that were used for the limited passenger service during the entire life of the Tharsis operation was photographed at Corrales on the same occasion. (D.Trevor Rowe)

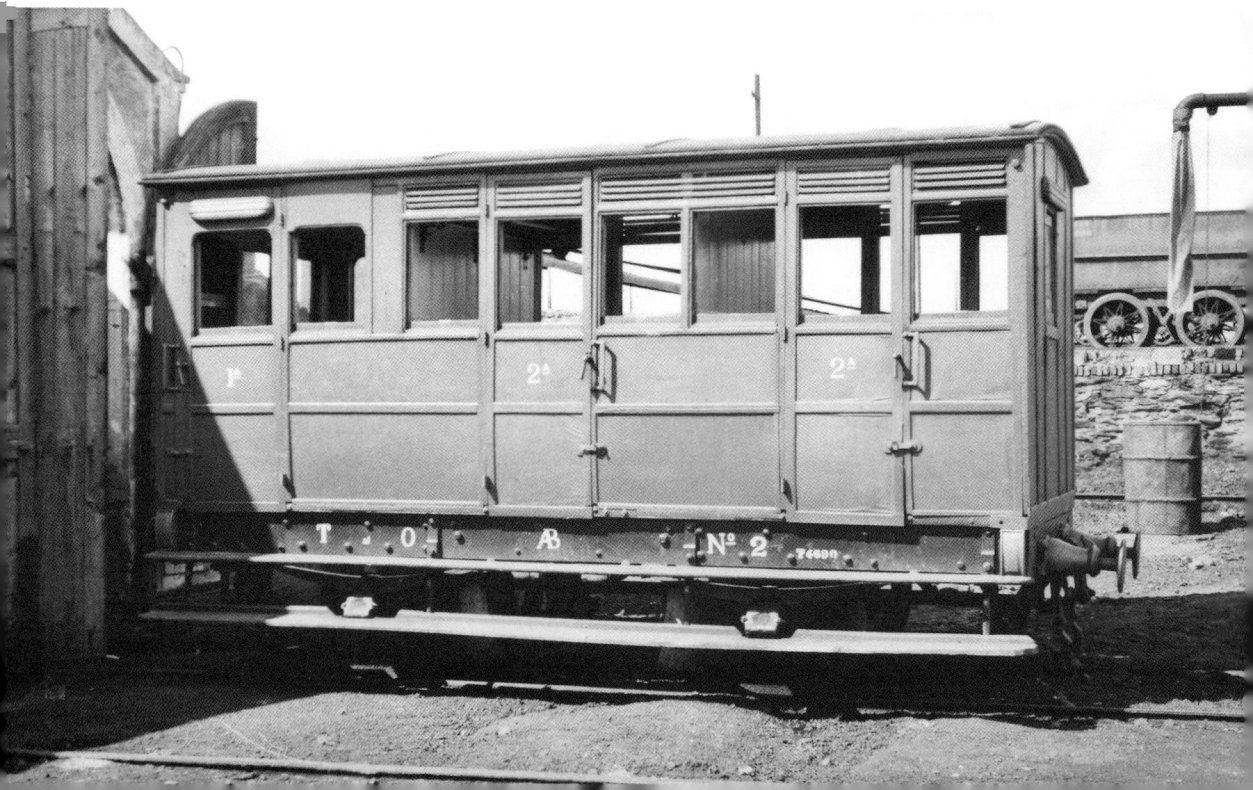

5.29.   For much of its active life, the Tharsis line relied on a fleet of powerful eight coupled locomotives to haul its heavy freight trains. One of the last to be supplied in 1955 was North British 0-8-0T no.53. Named *Hecca*, this impressive machine was recorded at Corrales on 25th April 1962. (D.Trevor Rowe)

5.30.   Fitted with a Giesl Ejector, Hohenzollern 2-8-0T no.41 *Alosno* was viewed on the turntable at Corrales depot on 23rd September 1963. (D.Trevor Rowe)

5.31. Hohenzollern 2-8-0T no. 39 *Tharsis* was witnessed departing northwards from Corrales with a load of empty wagons on the same occasion. Note the externally fitted wheels of the wagons and the closely spaced twin buffers of the locomotive. (D.Trevor Rowe)

5.32.   The once weekly passenger service during the later years consisted of a single carriage attached to the rear of the wagons. Hohenzollern 2-8-0T no.38 *Chanza* was in charge of such a working when it was viewed on 23rd September 1963. (D.Trevor Rowe)

5.33.   The final steam locomotive was supplied in 1955. North British 0-8-0T no.55 *Cerrejon* was recorded near Tharsis with a rake of empty wagons bound for the mines at La Zarza on 25th April 1962. (D.Trevor Rowe)

5.34.   Supplied in 1905, this North British 0-6-0T no.31 *El Cerro* was in excellent condition when it was photographed at Tharsis on the same day. (D.Trevor Rowe)

5.35.   North British 0-8-0T no.51 *Juncalejo* was pictured as it passed through Tharsis Emplalme, whilst hauling another rake of empty wagons on 25th April 1962. (D.Trevor Rowe)

5.36.   The largest of the mines served by the railway was at La Zarza, situated at the northern extremity of the network. Giesl Ejector fitted North British 0-8-0T no.52 *Gua* was viewed whilst being refuelled and serviced at the depot, prior to hauling a train down the line to Puntal de la Cruz on 23rd January 1965. (J.Wiseman)

CONCLUSION

Although, with one exception, all the narrow gauge lines featured in this volume have now closed, Spain still has much to offer the railway traveller. The modern RENFE network is one of the finest in Europe and is equipped with some superbly equipped and comfortable trains. With Madrid at the centre of the system, innumerable permutations are available for the intrepid enthusiast to cover many of the regions covered in this publication. Museums containing items relating to some of the former narrow gauge railways are located at Zaragoza and the Río Tinto mining complex.

Inter-Rail passes and other vital information relating to rail travel in the country can be obtained from:

Ffestiniog Travel, 6 Snowdonia Business Park, Minffordd, Gwynedd, LL48 6LD
Tel: 01766 772050

MP **Middleton Press**

EVOLVING THE ULTIMATE RAIL ENCYCLOPEDIA

Easebourne Lane, Midhurst, West Sussex.
GU29 9AZ Tel:01730 813169

www.middletonpress.co.uk email:info@middletonpress.co.uk
A-978 0 906520 B- 978 1 873793 C- 978 1 901706 D-978 1 904474 E- 978 1 906008

All titles listed below were in print at time of publication - please check current availability by looking at our website - *www.middletonpress.co.uk* or by requesting a Brochure which includes our *LATEST* RAILWAY TITLES also our TRAMWAY, TROLLEYBUS, MILITARY and WATERWAYS series